Advance Praise for
American Saunter

American Saunter is an abecedarian dance across the United States. From Gettysburg to Graceland, from Appalachia to the Redwoods, from Mothman to the Dalai Lama, Hayden catalogs American culture with photos and poems that echo both the joy and despair of our modern lives. With prayers like "umbilical cords," these powerful, open-voiced poems are just what America has been needing.

—**Cathryn Essinger**, author of *The Apricot and the Moon*

…what has struck me most about A.M. Hayden's work has been the role that nature plays in her use of language. As the title implies, *American Saunter* is pure Americana, a travelogue of the human spirit dedicated to this absurd, complicated country that many of us call home. Hayden's words explore what makes us laugh, what divides us, and what brings us back together, leaving us singing our own anthem under these endlessly wandering stars.

—**John Dorsey**, author of *Pocatello Wildflower*

Hayden does not just politely unwrap the gift of poetry to save the paper, but wholeheartedly tears the box apart with her teeth. She is a talented writer, but the most impressive thing to me is her fearlessness. She declares, "I love the sea!" then builds a boat, raises the sail, chooses a star, and sails across the ocean. She is an imagistic, insightful, emotional, and compelling poet; a rare bird who has genuinely reaffirmed what I love about poetry.

—**Jamey Dunham**, author of I*ntroduction to the Prose Poem* and *The Bible of Lost Pets*, Crashaw Prize winner

When I was a teenager, I hitchhiked from coast to coast, and from the north to south. It was one of the best times of my life. This is the essence of *American Saunter*. Hayden has captured an America that exists hidden like coins waiting between worn dinner cushions. Her words invite us to travel with her through all the myriad hues that exist just off the expressways, pooling in the places that flash by as we efficiently cruise control past. I thought I knew America, but Hayden has provided the ultimate travel guide in poetry.

—**Angela Yuriko Smith**, Two-time Bram Stoker Award® winner
and author of *Tortured Willows*

In *American Saunter*, we join Hayden on a cross-country exploration of the United States. Her evocative poems create a sense of place and longing. This exquisite and powerful poetry collection took me to places of my dreams, familiar yet transformed.

—**Teresa Berkowitz**, Editor-In-Chief, *Tangled Locks Journal*

With her compelling photographs and musicality of language, A.M. Hayden provides both the scenery and the soundtrack for this poetic journey. *American Saunter* braids personal and shared landscapes in a collection that feels both grand and intimate. And just as we become comfortable in the space where Hayden's imagery has us firmly rooted, ancient voices, ever protective of place, reach through these poems reminding us to tread lightly, reminding us that we are merely "a drop of water / restrained in the cactus / simmering on a snake's split tongue."

—**Aimee Noel**, Educator/Poet,
Ohio Arts Council Excellence Award winner

AMERICAN SAUNTER

POEMS OF THE U.S.

FLOWERSONG
PRESS

poetry by

A.M. Hayden

FLOWERSONG
PRESS

FlowerSong Press
Copyright © 2024 by A.M. Hayden
ISBN: 978-1-963245-49-3

Published by FlowerSong Press
in the United States of America.
www.flowersongpress.com

Image Credits:

Southwest Road (Cochiti Pueblo): Vasiliki Alexopoulos

Mothman (Point Pleasant Pantoum): Photo by A.M. Hayden,
Edited by Kris Coffey/Douglas Sovonick

Kiva (Kiva in New Mexico) by the author, edits by Kris Coffey.

Pride (Pride in Portland…): C. Heling-Bauer, Edited by A.M. Hayden

All Other Photography: A.M. Hayden

Cover Image by A.M. Hayden

Cover Design by Douglas Sovonick

Set in Adobe Garamond Pro

NOTICE: SCHOOLS AND BUSINESSES
FlowerSong Press offers copies of this book at quantity discount with bulk purchase
for educational, business, or sales promotional use. For information, please email the
Publisher at info@flowersongpress.com.

For my Dad,
who taught me how to fly

Credits

A Barbaric Yawp and thank you to the editors and publications who first featured these poems:

- Voices of Real Anthology (Poetry is Life Press), "No Such Thing as a Woke White Woman"
- Green Shoe Sanctuary, "Oklahoma Tornado, Broken Hoop"
- Red Noise Collective, "Chaco Canyon"
- Anti-Heroin Chic, "Boy in Montana"
- Gyroscope Review, "Sex Appeal of an El Camino"
- Exercise Your Writes, "Snuff Clouds in South Carolina"
- Stripes Literary Magazine, "Biloxi"
- Crosswinds Poetry Journal, "Dayton Flood, 1913"
- Ohio Bards Anthology, "Ultralight over the Mississippi River"
- Rowayat, "Umbrellas and Crosses"
- Southern Quill, "Cochiti Pueblo Corn Dance"
- Yellow Arrow Publishing, "Rachel Carson National Wildlife Refuge"
- Cosmic Daffodil Journal, "Grand Canyon" and "Ode to an Ohio Prairie"
- Songs of Wild Ohio, "Ode to an Ohio Prairie" (second publication)
- Willows Wept Review, "Big Bend National Park" and "Kiva in New Mexico"
- Ohio Pride Event, "Pride in Portland"
- Flights Magazine, "Snuff Clouds in South Carolina" and "Questions of Soul Surfing"
- Flora Fiction, "Mesa Verde"
- Hope Springs Anthology (Simple Simons Press), "Watching Ukraine"*
- Carnation Collection (Wild Ink Publishing), "American Priestesses"

- Slipstream Press, "Red Nashville"
- Echoes of the Wild Anthology, "Whale Watching off the Coast of Maine"
- Paradox Lit, "Rinse, Repeat, Chalkboard"
- Northern Appalachian Review, "Loretta Lynn at the Grand Ole Opry"
- When the River Speaks Anthology, "Redwoods"
- Of Our Own Accord Anthology (Flying Ketchup Press), "Rachel Carson National Wildlife Refuge" (second publication) and "Zora Neale Hurston!"
- The Poet's Billow, "On Losing your Childhood Home in Illinois"**

*Pushcart Prize Nominee

**Bermuda Triangle Prize Finalist

table of contents

Content Warning:

Some poems contain adult language and/or deal with themes of assault, violence and sexual violence, school shootings, genocide, colonization, war, mental health, animal and parental loss, death, suicide, and grief.

Please take care.

AMERICAN SAUNTER

"People ought to saunter---Do you know the origin of that word 'saunter?' It's a beautiful word. Away back in the Middle Ages people used to go on pilgrimages to the Holy Land, and when people in the villages through which they passed asked where they were going, they would reply, 'A la sainte terre,' 'To the Holy Land.' And so, they became known as sainte-terre-ers or saunterers."

—**John Muir**

American Priestess

spiraled prayer lifts discreet edges of bare feet
   weaves story and song through Demeter's Forest
      mother-daughter-sister-goddess celestial phases
      of waxing, full, and hard-won waning
         winds down to the creek, the prairie
            to create ceremony of sweet alyssum, sage clary,
              lavender water, woody ash
           place grained Persephone palms to earth
      bowed like willows seeking water, speaking to the taproot
to heal wounds, unfurl the knots
    untwist tangles of trauma
      banish-the-invasive-which-strives-viciously-to-take-up-residence,
         to reclaim, sanctify multi-hued sacred dwellings
           ancestral villages, holy temples, feminine bodies
        built with strong, fortified bones
       weathered hands, hematite heart scars
     cedar sprig thick braids and nectar
   shapeshifters into alchemists sing
     solstice trill: *hold me, sisters*
       tinctured tongues baptized
          in medicinal Midsummer

Arkansas Gospel Haiku

Take time for Jesus
Fred's flag-shaped belt buckle read
He took time for you

Big Bend National Park, Texas

1.

roadrunners look nothing
like the cartoon
far smaller against creosote
bushes and yucca
no *meep meeps*

2.

sundried canyon walls
tower sides of the Rio Grande
as we surrender supine to
fresh packed mud floor
gaze vertical to imaginary
hot air balloons
left leg and arm to U.S.
right leg and arm to Mexico
for a moment, a bridge

3.

Emory Peak summit
across *Chisos, ghost, phantom*
mountains, last
stronghold of the toughest Apache
people of the forest

4.

blooming rainbow, prickly pear
strawberry pitaya cactus
red and yellow desert roses on
braille lids of spiked canteens

bide out the rains, restraint
Native American Church
peyote buttons
steeped in tea, consumed
never smoked
pipe across open pages of the Bible
for a moment, a bridge

5.

Santa Elena Canyon
four months parched
sky whistles *O*
into uncovered mouth
cloud torrents pour
between two mesas
two materialized *RoyGBiv de bows*
impeccable *wax-ons*, all the way
for a moment, a bridge
what does it mean?

6.

all roads end
at the Rio Grande
arroyos can shapeshift
into raging rivers
while you sleep

7.

Mexican long-nosed bats,
copperheads, four species of
venomous rattlesnakes
coiled assassins in
clay crannies and crumble nooks
"snakes, scorpions, and tarantulas
generally won't hurt you unless you
*annoy them"**
same, snakes, scorpions, and
tarantulas

8.

Hikers leave two traces
of Texarkana drawls in their wake
one gallon water jugs
strapped like Bjorn's to concave chests
sweet, liquid, life-saving babies
a camera clicks, the dark-haired one
leans closer, swathed in sagebrush
notes of solid shoulders
boy on edge of man

9.

vultures turn lazy circles
to Tori Amos songs on repeat
indigo and violet
Chihuahuan waves
ancient tree squats
gnarled roots twist
wicked branches point
to the horizon

10.

you choke on an exhale of tears
from the sapphire streak
of spirit voltage
you, held in open cupped palms
in basin's hypnotic heartbeat
8,000 feet of infinity
surges through each cell
for a moment, a bridge

Big Bend National Park Service Pamphlet, 1999

Big Chicks in Chicago

Start with Al Capone
      sing sing sing
at the Green Mill
      tall trombone
sweet eyed player
      whispers *yes yes yes*
full lips smile around each circular note
      another in skinny pants, mouths "let's dance"
elbows, forearms, knees fly and buzz like busy bees
      loose, suspended, jazz mended
we pass the tattoo shop where artists hand out
      watermelon blow pops after gauges
shake our hips by the Salsa club where the bewitched
      fever press together in rhythmic heat waves
on the way to the Clipper where rockabillies with new-school tattoos
      teeter and tap on cartoon-sized basses
pluck strings, jump and jive
      above duck tailed hair sweeps as we
slide our way to the final stage
      80s synthesizer in chockablock Day-Glo swing
surrender in a sea of Big Chicks
      gay men and our grand Madonna
in diamond glitter
      to hear you shout/whisper
I wish I felt this
      in waking life

Biloxi, Mississippi

Sand in your eye
is burning glass
distorted splinter
scraping against the silk
of your ocean sight
the warning
a reminder
to trust
your intuition
whimpering
under their clammy
penny-tasting palm
clamped over
your voice
held hostage for years
and when they spit
in your face
screaming
You're giving up on love
by leaving me
you blink out the shards
onto the crinkly plastic
restrained over the hotel bed's
filthy mattress
you pry their knuckles off
spit out the gristle and grit
between your teeth
and tongue
use your own strong fingers
to sweep, claw at your mouth
clear the debris,

the broken teeth
as you howl, *No*
I would be giving up on love
if I stayed

Blue Ridge Mountains Swami

Unzip leaking tent   pooling with rain   stumble out, yawn
     to meditation hall   veiled in   silence and   layered fog
green trees   protect themselves   from dripping heat   become pigeon
     blue ridges   rise from vanishing   shadows   scattered
     azure haze   low *whhhizzz* passes   on your left   sherbet
robe snaps   whips into   flame   trailing blinking
red light   guide   to morning   prayers   crisscross   applesauce
     Swami   on a bicycle   ghost   in the mist

Boy in Montana

He wonders what it was all for
the momentary, still haunting fire
his anarchist anti-conformist
punk-is-not-dead   skate   lungs

nightmares and bizarre daydreams
stories inked into flesh, skulls, and teeth
of what lies beneath
shadows, knives, and creatures
formidable angels too
because his wings tremble at   the   boy
he pretends to ignore

She wonders what it was all for
on a cigarette run, doc martens
propped up on   his   glovebox
if she would have
whispered *yes*
under the fluorescents
when their faces leaned close
would their ache for each other
have granted   real   asylum

from the feeble, sadistic
fowler's snare concealed at
the next corner
set to groom and carve
an unguarded, fledgling girl's
untouched body, systematically
slicing her all directions
until she staggered wounded in   strips,   tatters

They wonder what it was all for
if their nascent pull, eager and sincere
would have been a talisman
against the violent nightmare or   bizarre daydream

Scarecrow mystery or   suicidal tendency

Brooklyn

We are clatter birds
click clack claws on cobblestone
in new Manhattan

Cancelled Due to Lack of Interest

Workshop: "Finding God in the Stories of Our Lives"

Cancelled   due to lack of interest
We apologize   *for the Inconvenience*

Chaco Canyon

Do not disturb the rocks
      of the ancient Anasazi canyon
            loud with spirits, old to new
                  east to west, sun to moon

A few fools pretend
      to be foxes
            with deep pockets
                they are not

Falcon spirits follow
      down the powdery road
            curl ethereal smoke talons
                under false fox tires

Lemmings should
      not wear fox masks
            and should *never*
                disturb the rocks

Chickens in Kansas

and they all join in, celebrating with her
as she adds her proud egg to shared straw nest
she alerts her loud "buhgawk" first

and they all join in, celebrating with her
each of their "buhgawk' a "get it, sister!"
hens lifting up hens, "Yes, girl, yes!"

and they all join in celebrating with her
as she adds her proud egg to shared straw nest

Cincinnati Train Station

"I'll miss you," she grasps
"Me too," he loosens, a limp claw machine
who keeps the car idling while she unloads
her backpack, holds her arms out to him
his weak squeeze and release
a vapor that dissipates before she can seek
the heat his chest always heaped on hers
"See you in two weeks," he slinks
back into driver's side
hustles away from the curb in the night
she stares at the taillights
of his stupid car
lifts her chin to the moonrise
1:08 station clock, 2 a.m. to Brooklyn
push it down, what is falling apart
ignore learning in class last week a dark
placenta means something is stirring
even stretching the absence would kickstart
his heart, midwife his intoxicating
barrage of breathy promises he lavishly
ladled into her parted mouth days before
his entangled arms and legs binding her
into him, forming new edges of her shape,
remembering back further to early gig days
when his friend had leaned in close to warn,
he lies as much to himself
as he lies to the girls he's with
and now, 1:23 a.m. she loathes
the indifferent, suspended titan eye of
truth unraveling "they" like a chewed mixtape
glowering witness to their death rattle

City Lights, San Francisco

Do not kid yourself, these are not novels, they are mind-altering, eye opening, creative surges, passionate, ransack photographs of bohemian wanderlust, spun diaries of Zen lunatics wild and raw, soul records of crazy revelations, dizzy desires, strange creatures, wacked visions, and souvenir stories, tangible on your tonsils against American terrain, unfamiliar transient faces, dusty sunsets ablaze, hepcats and holy flowers, bop nights and kink jazz supernovas, fanciful dreams, chaotic adventures, stimulation, alienation, atonement, at-one-ment, sleep deprivation, disorientation, experience of deep mysteries, visions, and epiphanies, bounce from one town to next, east to west, no guarantees, miracles could happen any moment, wonderous spontaneity, haunted with travel, far away from home, no home, the world is home, but not really, between worlds, days last weeks, months last days, tattered notebook, pen, and starry skies to fill the insides, gritty soundtrack of rumble trains gateway to freedom, guttural midnight horn a call to liberation, strangers become friends become strangers, surrender to divine beat, buzz of life, in love with every new face, new sensation, new word, each one satisfies like small storms in bone dry mouths, only those who *explode like roman candles,* only those whose lives run parallel for a short sacred while, only those who discover the rattlesnake enlightenment America aches for, all she holds, feeds, punishes, liberates, all absurd, within us all, a collective diary with skeleton key to unlock for whoever tumbles out the toadstool any given magic moment

Cochiti Pueblo Corn Dance

Lightning flare paints the landscape
Southwest shock knockout
Galvanized turquoise skies
Clouds cast giant sea shadows
Follow the gravel, chalky miles to a covert
Pueblo circle of dancers in textured regalia
Feathers for Feast Day
Velvety moccasins press into
Baked terrain to drum heartbeats

Woman with silver-tongued discs
Woven into her braids, memory rivers
Carved down her face, leans in
Murmurs like a secret
We dance to ask Great Spirit for a good maize harvest
Corn, you know? We pray to the corn deity

Deep breath umbilical cord prayers shapeshift ceremony
Artists at tables, stalls, and tents
Writers, poets, storytellers, multi-colored beaded necklaces
Silver hair ties, corn dolls, clay pottery calligraphy
Cottonwood and aspen drums, stretched skin warm to the touch
Sand paintings, turquoise earrings, dangling dreamcatchers for tourists
Fry bread sincere and tender in open air
Stories deeper than cracks thirsting for rain, entrenched
Ancestor lines to the Revolt
Little dreamer corn seeds soar on Kachina wings
Good medicine

Days Inn Angel in Dastaar, Atlanta

three delays
several sapped hours
stuck on insipid tarmac
sweltering, unmoving plane
long limp of new jersey-sized
airport, shuttles shut down
4 a.m. stuck, bleary
blood sugar plummet
city purgatory

Sikh hotel clerk
royal blue turban
loam brown eyes
passes a glass of nearly
cool milk over the counter,
one unpeeled banana, barely
bruised, a partially
unwrapped bean burrito
from the Taco Bell
across the street
always open

Dayton Flood, 1913

She watched
the flood waters
on 5th street
pour out of the
brick's second story
stained glass windows
now 19th century faucets
rivers parted
the kitchen's
creaky floor
revealing a bloated
waterlogged carcass
of what used
to be a horse
she looked out
the window
minus its glass
and recognized
her upright piano
nod up and down
the narrow alleyway
into the street
past the neighbor's backyard
as the murky water carried
the instrument further away
she couldn't help
but think to herself,
Thank God,
now I don't have to take
any more piano lessons

Gettysburg

never written on the back of an envelope
272 appropriate words
to assure this ground could not be hallowed

sssshhhhhh clump sssshhhhhh clump
her shovel blades loosen dirt
limp bonnet hangs over her sweat-drenched neck
soiled apron wraps her pregnant belly
wax paper protects swishing salmon
she digs
buries one body at a time

silence
thunder cracked for three days
over the ridge and fields
echoed through woods, across creeks
drenched crests of hills, rang behind barns
washed up and down fence lines
Wheatfield and Cemetery Hill
Peach Orchard and Plum Run
Oak Ridgeline and Devil's Den
each place where grass gills
pressed flat under boot
while expanse of camouflaged fields
flapped and waved
soldiers lined like hooked lures
red fish, blue fish

Graceland

she brings you to tears
young Priscilla so lovely
you forget cocaine
mirrored rooms, shag jade carpet
mounting floors to the ceiling

Grand Canyon

1.
Thirst
it always comes back
to water in wilderness sun

2.
baked sculpture
slow progress
in whose mind?
150 million malleable
years of *wu-wei*
soft overcomes hard
flexible over rigid
rock paper scissors
water beats rock

3.
dusty zipper switchbacks
Zig zag zig up down up
cracked drought rivers
layer after layer

4.
no blue as blue as this blue
lapis quivers between
white winged weightless
fluffball cotton giants
cast dark cobalt shadows
across infinite ridges
deep as lakes, dive in
desert mirages

5.
vapor limbs extend
to peaks like vulture shadows
swirls of scattered bones and spirits
roam in the wind
carried in mouths of panting lizards

6.
sweaty backs lean
on surprisingly cool walls
breeze whispers relief
lifts wisps of hair
off necks, ruffles
feathers of hawks

7.
Hualapai live inside
and Navajo (Dine)
Beauty before, beauty behind
beauty all around, beauty in all
and Havasupai
who proclaim, *we are the Grand Canyon*
no more "Indian" Garden

8.
always use caution
mules have right away
press your backpack flush, uphill side
stand statue still
do not talk or fidget
hooves loosen small rocks

who disappear off the sides
wait another sixty feet
a spooked mule is certain injury
and backpackers can be assholes

9.
Hair snaps into knives
at Plateau Point
view smeared with gauzy
marmalade lens, golden citrus
folds and unfolds
heavy, solid, liquid
luminated like a headdress
of cactus flowers with lace ribbons
floating down to Colorado's curve
ridged rooftop to *sound your
Barbaric Yawp!*

10.
Naked canyon floor
river laps over bruised feet *yin*
surges at bend *yang*

11.
Deer, birds, lizards
snakes, scorpions
shake out your boots
and your sleeping bag
every time

12.
Agave flowers grow
one foot a day
these are not canyons
they are earth cathedrals
chiseled by cherry cotton

scaled by thousands of sculptured
staircases
formed into sherbet phantom
hawk rock pinatas

13.
Ascension
takes twice as long
is where you
get into trouble
do not ever forget
you are a drop of water
restrained in the cactus
simmering on a snake's split tongue

Haystack Rock, Oregon Coast

                    Hay
              stack rock pirate
           map mouth, booby traps
           piano keys, bicycles, basalt
         sea stack fill your pockets with
         puffins real gold treasures, Oregon   *for*
wildlife   Islands marine refuge good enough   *me*

How to Eat a Lobster in New Hampshire

1.

If you have enough money (probably not, but *you are on vacation*, you deserve it!) order a Lobster (pre-boiled out of sight).

2.

Press down the small nutcracker tool hard for the CRAACK.

3.

Flip the clawless carcass over to bend the back into a bridge, snap that tail off.

4.

Bend the tiny flippers, dolphin like, until they separate with the sound of finality.

5.

Insert the shiny small trident placed neatly before you.

6.

Stick the fork good and in there, apply pressure to split in half, revealing the greenish delicacies.

7.

For good measure, crack once more sideways. Now, enjoy! You have worked hard for this!

8.

Finally, return to the claws like a straw, suck out the meat until nothing is left.

9.

Sit back and sigh, slightly disgusted, but satisfied, butter brush aside any small pangs of guilt that arise.

10.

Don't hold gaze with their black, seedy eyes. Desensitize.

Kids in America

locked in a vice grip
as we wave our kids to school
a local child filled
with 46 entrance wounds
this is our America

Kiva in New Mexico

We can climb 140 feet up to cliff dwellings among rugged tree tops
we can climb down into the intact round kiva

does not mean we should
descend the ladder through the small opening, *shipapu*

pass the *park sign:* identical replica, still holds same
ceremonial space, same stillness inside

council meetings, Kachina songs, prayers, decisions
we sit on cool ground, lean against quiet wall, close our eyes, breathe in, breathe out

abrupt shouts from above snap us like rubber bands, eyes fly open
stampede of screams, toothpick and sausage legs with sweaty sponge arms storm the *shipapu*

thimble feet tear and kick up sifted sand settled for centuries
disturbed breath, cells, skin of ancients spiral on our lips, in our lungs

curt shout from above, clearly in charge, "Let's GO!"
as quickly as they came, windmill arms, feet and squeals scramble back up

leaving scattered spirit hymnals knocked off earth pews
they whisper strongly: *You should not be here. You should not be here.*

Knitting Socks in Iowa

She   unravels

          yarn's

        stitched   secrets

           hidden in

                  stinging

              winter

                    wind

Loretta Lynn at the Grand Ole Opry

Her Daddy's daughter
raises her
formidable palm
up to Jesus first
then to her fans
under Ryman's spotlights
her ivory dress shimmers
like diamonds in the dew
her butterbean voice sweeps
to smooth my hair
kiss the crown of my head
breathe in deeply
the way I will
with my daughters
a decade from now
depths of faith
from Butcher Holler
How Great Thou Art
her voice breaks
as she rolls over
 "Oh My God"
like holy waters
my heart halts
into a country fist
as I imagine her
spinning circles
bare feet in wet grass
beneath Johnny Cash's
window at 3 a.m.
an Appalachian apparition

Lorraine Motel, Memphis

Dexter Avenue to Mulberry Street
not one hair of one head would be harmed
no matter how great the provocation   how great that provocation

in one sepia photo, he leans
over his lawn fence, next to his young son
pulls up, maybe barbed wire   how many seconds

to bring into focus this
weighty wooden cross
charred black, still in embers   places have power

he pulled back his motel sheets
that morning, still rumpled
frozen in time, stained coffee mugs   near the balcony

a grey pigeon limps his left wing
pecking, scraping along the railing
no world house vision, how many minutes   before Coretta knew?

had he visited local halls to play pool?
to straddle the table, take a keen shot
behind his back, he was good at that   8-ball corner pocket

tear-stained visitors
amble in slow motion
pinballs in molasses   every face damp

Mansfield, Missouri
Home of Laura Ingalls Wilder

It may be *this*
weathered case propping up Pa's gallant fiddle
or her assertion they *could not*
have survived as a family without it

It may *be*
the compact kitchen fitted with low cabinets and
countertops custom built by Manly for Laura's 4'10 frame
just imagine her skirt shuffling as she opened and
closed drawers hunting for the teaspoon
she had *forgotten*

It may be *because*
she wrote on 5-cent school tablets with pencils
she sharpened in between pages of grasshopper clouds
pancake men, small fingers frozen from twisting hay
in stinging cold of long winter's blizzard

It may be the front porch
of this sweet house under its ashen roof
knowing she stood right here in this
timbered spot we stand in *now*

Or maybe it *is*
the chimney Manley built with his steady
close-set eyes, one stone at a time
which still ascends rock solid into *now*

Or maybe *it*
is their white shiplap home itself built one room at a time
like her books like our lives
it must be her writing desk wooden, humble

near the square window
where one *can*
overlook their Ozark orchard

Or it may be because they *never*
drove a car until Rose bought them one
and despite her success, somehow it is difficult
to care about Rose
it feels more sincere to *be*

wholly devoted to Laura
and our Laura does not drive *a*
Buick

And maybe we resent Rose for leading
her folks down the *long*
lane to the freshly built Rock House
far away from Laura's low cozy cabinets,
little wooden desk, lined yellow tablets

Or it may be how Laura knew well
it is a beautiful world, also, when it is *time*
to let scratching of pencil fall silent
for sole purpose of listening
to the gathering of blackbirds
cackling in cacophony outside a window
to marvel when hundreds of steadfast
wings lift into one wedded *whoosh*
taking her breath away
and ours too, one
holy moment
a century *ago*

"*This could not be forgotten because now is now…it can never be a long time ago.*"
Little House in the Big Woods, Harper and Brothers, 1932

Mesa Verde, Colorado

mud mortar, build your kivas first (21 kivas, 150 rooms)
sifted smooth city steps weave vertical, friendly snakes wind up
narrow and steep, *you can still touch* the plaster families slept against
800 years ago, what cliff lullabies did their kids dream this high,
under nightscape and cosmos' brilliance, explosion of stars,
constellation stories, *you can still touch* original holds for their hands and toes
to climb out the tunnels, life and death, you crawl, become a four-legged
no longer two-legged, like in the *inipi*
sweat lodge womb
if there were ancient Anasazi baby gates
to keep kids from falling the brochure does not say, but a parent wonders, also not
mentioned,
the common mistake of saying Indigenous peoples had *no civilization*
when 21 kivas are 21 churches
and we know by this, we are in the footsteps of those who understood *be still and know*
without it written in ancient scrolls, who knew how to collect water from seep springs
and carve channels in bedrock, how to rip mighty echoes through the canyon
to the horizon, to their ancestors, whose shoulders were smooth with wings
in ancient worlds, who knew how to celebrate and gather
to leave messages and poems, track moon cycles, anticipate eclipses
how to craft individual blocks of sandstone to stack fortified walls
in the sides of towering cliffs,
civilized people who knew
for 700 years
how to be families
how to protect their kids so they could
safely dream under the nightscape,
create stellar narratives, become constellations

Me Too (apartment, party, alley, street, bedroom, loft, dorm, basement, car, anywhere, everywhere, USA)

TW: Sexual Assault/Violence

Look to light, lotus writhe through tangled muck, surface from silence, gasp for air, born from bondage, fear of *judgment triggers retaliation blame* when you dig into your pain, they question *timing memory credibility complicity* as anger wound securely around your spool of survival starts to unravel in convulsive bursts, shushed doors opened to lace trimmed *Holly Hobbie* curtains hanging limply over faded pink bedspread, older family member's hushed *Don't tell anyone* freezing hands sneaking down a 10-year-old's corduroys, afraid of getting in trouble and it was not your fault, violently expelling dark death-metal doors to fowler snaring a teenaged girl, daring her to do dangerous deeds, priming her for his perilous assails, calling her *coward* when she says *stop,* he sneers, *time to grow up* pins legs and arms, hand clamped over mouth, slashed down her middle, just like that she is snatched from youth, exiled, not by some dark alley stranger, but someone who said *I love you,* someone who had hunted before, and it was not your fault, doors wretch open to weedy wrist grabber, brake slammer, shoves her into wall, spits across eyes squeezed shut, says *I love you, never again* until more screaming, chasing, forcing face into abrasive, sour carpet, caging her under thrifted table, rolling to trap under his full weight, squeezing jaw, pain surprising, shocking even and she cannot breathe, hands constrict throat, no recognition in these malevolent eyes, we'd choose the bear every time, and it occurs to her *this is how it happens,* and he follows her to apartments, parking lots, vulture's librettos of unhinged rage disguised as epic devotion, and she walks with keys pointed out, clenched tightly, like her breath, and it was not your fault, people make poison, strangers too, kite-high night alley ghost who skulked 5th street's shadows to screech vile vulgarities to her back while she ran, ran, ran, throat parched from panting, and big boot guy at the party yanking up her shirt's hem to shove his lit cigarette into her bellybutton, how thirty years later, she still can feel its blinding burn refusing to extinguish no matter how freezing the tap water poured in, it was not your fault because ask a survivor, *When?* the answer likely is, *Which time?*

and it *cannot* be this way for your daughters, years of mental gymnastics to conjure some *why* that makes sense, shame of paralysis to *prevent it stop it* and it was not your fault, your daughters will know their worth, they will *not* be taught to endure, they will not be conditioned to *put up with it,* and it was not your fault, your mind endlessly twists all angles to forget, but your body remembers when midwife sweeps your dilating cervix, a muscle connective tissue pull chain uncoils a piercing, primal shriek two decades buried by phantom hands, eclipse of totality, darkest moment momentarily blocking brightest one, stunning how this happens, and it was not your fault, whether you had to stay silent, camouflage to hide, sacrifice truth to survive, no matter *what* you were told, you are *not* damaged goods, please listen, beloved, what was done to you does *not* define you, dear daughter, it was not your fault

New York City 1
(Advice to a Midwesterner)

They warned, do *not* say
hi or smile at anyone
or you will get a
Fuuuuuck you, buddy in return
a New York welcome

New York City 2
("Queen of "Foreigners")

Pieces carried across plum Atlantic
Lenape Island, foot in broken shackle
copper torch burning sky, Lady Liberty
sways in breeze, stone eyes to seven seas
threshold guardian, gracious giant gargoyle
brackish spiked crown, lightning scarred Majesty

New York City 3
("You talk fine")

!!!!!ELECTRI----
CITY!!!!!

Cue

Carly

Simon music
poems   perpetually

slick

fashioned

into peacoats

and parkas

sparkling   in
New

Jerusalem

57

Niagara Falls

drenched thundering roar
spray fury clapped prayers dive
for kosher hot dogs

No Such Thing as a Woke White Woman, Alabama

raised with the "n" word
fluent in "I'm not
a racist, but" vernacular
messages stacked into

matryoshka dolls of
prejudiced memory
layers of differentiation
how to initiate reconciliation

to find the string,
unravel this othering, is
America due for a new
Great Awakening

from faith's spiritual sedation
and propagation to obey
do as they say, *hush,* while
they paint Jesus with a

narrow, white paintbrush
secret pockets of oral storytelling
ancestor divination, bodily volition
spirit dance, ring shouts

power in God, the liberator
not the Pharoah, not the preacher
last shall be first, first shall be last
Christ as radical, rebel, and black

emancipation from Egypt
exodus of freedom
conceived in those spirit meetings
because there is no such thing

as a woke white woman

when down below
stained abrasive robes
buried in the ink leathered satchel
found in a crawlspace in Alabama

plain cardboard, flimsy and flat
shapes those hateful hats
how slight the sinister sheaths
small men crept behind

how to recognize a
history dehumanized
oversexualized, despised, animalized
to a revolution, revelation, elucidation

instead of being "woke"
we can be a lantern at our shins
illuminating history's sins
witness with a clearer lens

to scare demons out of every crawlspace
is it such a sacrifice
because apology does not suffice
we must learn this perversive history

no more willful amnesia or complicity
acknowledge when racism is systemic
where to begin with reconciliation? let's
start by withdrawing "woke" from our vocab

affirm I am listening
I am leaning into the truth
as much as I can, story by story
I will be open, I am...
because there is no such thing
as a woke white woman

or a woke, white man

No Volvere Amor Mio (Tri-State Tea Readings)

How we hold the future in our palms, juvenescent
and invincible as Greek myths reflected in Tarot
and Turkish tea readings, sleeping under *open
sky of crystal silence*, Seven of Cups
pouring dream luminescence

whispered words coil up into vapor, nearly mystic
double helix, discussing dinner's shared fortune
cookie, whose slip spoke: *true love is like ghosts*

ghost ghazal steeped through ginger tea, red
velvet staircase pressed to black dress, two white
chrysanthemums pulled from your coat pocket

encountering God's infinite indigo wildness
standing in the kitchen window's moonlight

who is the Alchemist, turning static to ocean waves?

How we dance, symphony supercharged
Farsi-Arabic-Spanish-Scales, melodies moving
into swift gust-carried stir of embers
fanned into a bolero flame, rumba of acoustic
rhythms, Arvo Part, Voodoo of Stan Getz and Neruda

new Millenium and cracked doumbek, taped
back together like your woodwork thick wrists
all chakras as solar plexus, all fruit as dessert

are we the rattlesnake riders, *soleil* and *mauchtaub?*
locked eyes holding what is ancient as desert sand,
time poised on sliver of our next carnation breaths

frame the dried roses, encircle the words speaking to this
taste of brilliant *joie de vivre* that was as real as anything

poets with sugar dripping from our tongues

Ocean of Wisdom in an Indiana Cornfield

All eyes follow the slow-moving, maroon-swathed living bodhisattva, buddha-to-be
His Holiness, the 14th Dalai Lama, Ocean of Wisdom

as he tucks the gathers of his robe with a humble squat onto the seated platform
among uniform rows of green and yellow corn in the Hoosier State

film cameras and Muhammad Ali at his side
biscuit and ghee, peanut butter and jelly
grassy field of middle- and upper-class dressed in khakis and wide-eyed ecstasy

palms folded in namaste, disenchanted with childhood faiths
desperately seeking exotic enlightenment or something like it

clustered near colored sand mandala tent, three little girls: one tall in corduroys,
next in pigtails with sunshine barrettes, last freckle-faced in sky-blue dress
all clasp hands, run in circles, fall, laugh, get up, run, fall, repeat

Samsara fits of giggles
as Nobel Peace Prize winner, spiritual leader of Tibet
Lhamo Thondup, renamed Tenzin Gyatso

reincarnation of Avalokiteshvara, bodhisattva of compassion
(good friend of Richard Gere and Muhammad Ali)

suggests to the eager audience, *do not worry about becoming Buddhists,*
instead, *be better Christians, Jews, or Muslims*
transmuting a thousand serene, knowing smiles into a face deflation collective

when he laughs, which is often, his cloaked shoulders
shake up and down, *ho ho ho,*
children still practicing pure dharma, oblivious to this Tibetan Santa

Ode to a St. Louis Drag Queen

You walk
No, sway
No, Swayze sashay

in painful, glorious heels
two spikes of pink bubblegum
hold your solid feet
swivel waist
blonde wig teased-for-the-gods

puff painted lips
glossy fuchsia edges lift

flash your toothy dazzle
against glistened onyx skin
you stumble and laugh loudly
hands arch, bent spoons at your wrists
cigarette dangles precariously
between your tapered, cranberry nails

coifed curse words and levity
padded promise and pardon

Ode to an Ohio Prairie

We walk through these wildflowers
in this sacred prairie
we talk to our ancestors
and listen for their stories

Singing nettles in nature's nave
thistle, clover, and ironweed
primordial prayers whispered
in wooly ears of drifting seed

Queen Anne's lace waves and calls,
curls her index finger to you in invitation
dancing blooms into September's hours
witness the first preservation

Do not hurry, saunter instead
you need not gaze far to be enchanted

Hold space for reverence and wonder
for infinite galaxies live in these fauna
multi-hued tapestries of splendor
golden cattails genuflect as if in Siena

Red-winged blackbirds are soothsayers
gargoyles of maple and walnut trees
weavers pluck their strings like violin players
milkweed a patchwork quilt of bees

Loam breath, explosion of sun prayer
spiritual pilgrim, *A la Sainte Terre*

No higher calling than steward
her aster lungs breathe
because we left her be
her cloister uncarved, *pu* in Tao speak

ever-bursting tonic of wildness
spilling over into eyes, lungs, and veins
compass of healing apothecary
chanted in cicadas' repeated refrains

Cathedral, mosque, synagogue, temple
What could transcend this creation miracle?

Oklahoma Tornado, Broken Hoop

Ripped up oaks, roofless houses, upturned trucks, fences in trees
a handful of buildings still stand, more crushed to pulp, buried under debris

sundry handfuls of history books continue to call massacres "battles"
hide manifest destiny's countless faces: deliberate-starvation-long face

spread-of-incurable-disease-spotted face, forced-removals-stone face
broken-treaties-betrayal face, *The Trail Where They Cried* survivors

Oklahoma dumping grounds, where tear-children-out-of-mothers'-arms face waits
steal kids to "residential schools" where mouths are taped shut, Native tongues silenced

hair sliced with assimilation guillotines
prayers beaten from tiny threadbare bodies, no burial for names

tossed in the mass grave of civilize, *white-man-ize,* identity genocide
generational trauma like funnel clouds of rolling thunder and Hitler

who loved a cowboy, wrote his valentine for *the Long Walk*
admired its "blueprint" for concentration camps, reservations for ghettos

and mass graves duplicates of Wounded Knee
where half a century before, U.S. soldiers rolled and stacked bodies

the same bodies whose spirits Ghost Danced in prayer hours earlier,
before the massacre, or "battle" if battles were fought by women and children

On Losing your Childhood Home in Illinois

This house is flooded
the roof has lifted
walls of memories
the only
room left
the paint is peeling
under popcorn ceiling
countless layers rolled
to cover unidentified
fear in her bones

this house is flooded
with the disco couple
and never sleeping infant
sliding to awkward adolescence
eating Valentine chocolate
parroting *The Princess Bride*
hill and valley twice the size
on a red sled in January, how it glowed
under the full moon
illuminating the future hill
where vows are broken for survival
a foot severed for escape
in its ground

youthful familiars
seasoned superstitions
summer bends in the water
frogs and cicadas in harmony
eerie in darkness

this house is flooded
Sunday morning blackbirds
sweep the echoed hallways
flap their soiled wings
carried in the current
one final resounding hum

Piasa (Pie-ah-Saw) Bird

Wait for it, your eyes are explorers along ribboned cliffs, Great River Road's Illini mysteries
to discover ghastly glimpse of scaly, fishtailed beast, a horned and taloned devourer of men
Painted moons before palefaces, a winged and fire-eyed *jeepers creepers* of ancients before me

Wait for it, your eyes are explorers along ribboned cliffs, Great River Road's Illini mysteries
Father Marquette and fur trader Joliette marveled at the frescoed flesh-eater in their damp diaries
It took one dream, shapeshifting sacrificial Chief, poisoned arrow ambush, warriors two by ten

Wait for it, your eyes are explorers along ribboned cliffs, Great River Road's Illini mysteries
to discover ghastly glimpse of scaly, fishtailed beast, a horned and taloned devourer of men

"Piasa" = Illini word for "devourer of men"

Point Pleasant Pantoum

maybe he was lonely, among the mines and factories, exiled and afraid
      standing smokestacks, seven feet high, with a ten-foot wingspan
men in black suits lingered in their dark sunglasses and Cadillacs for days
      hysterical sightings of a glowing red-eyed, furry, menacing Mothman

standing smokestacks, seven feet high, with a ten-foot wingspan
      hollers' grey-faced fuzzed humanoid perched atop the ammo dump
hysterical sightings of a glowing red-eyed, furry, menacing Mothman
      rumor had it, if startled, he'd fly straight up

hollers' grey-faced fuzzed humanoid perched atop the ammo dump
      men in black suits lingered in their dark sunglasses and Cadillacs for days
rumor had it, if startled, he'd fly straight up
      maybe he was lonely, among the mines and factories, exiled and afraid

Pride in Portland
For C

Do you know what you deserve? Love.
to feel safe, to *be* safe at home, in your neighborhood, at work

at your bar, a club, your refuge
to not walk on eggshells, also the levity to make mistakes

to not be the mouthpiece for all LGBT, Q, I, A, to say *yes, this is me* in all my
complexity, undiscovered caverns, and multi-hued skies within me

to never underestimate the strength it takes to lift everyone's bullshit put upon your
shoulders and heart, to never underestimate the ferocity it takes

to be alive because you will never please everyone anyway
people always got something to say, hold as your creed what they think and do

is *no part of you,* none of your beeswax, only a murky, artless reflection
of their own mythology; then *carpe diem* your way through all the knots and loops

you are the architect, the artist, the director, the lead, words matter,
reclaiming words matters when the elevator soundtrack is a broken record of less than

not legal, not protected, second-class, not worthy, did you know rainbows
are the visible vow, *like, old school divine promise* of protection, of hope

cessation of all previous darkness? did you know centuries of Indigenous wisdom uplift
two-spirits as seamless beauty and balance while the rest of humanity are left

halved and split? to stay whole - that is a super power
he-she-they-them-his-hers-theirs-him-we-us-you belong here

as you are
worthy, worthy, worthy

an alchemy of limbs, wings, lips, heart, you are ever transitioning
triple goddess phases of spiraling, waxing, full, waning

it is okay to say *I have changed my mind,* or *I have discovered something
about me,* or *I have realized it has been this way all along*

and to mean it, your best revenge is to live your life whole in worthiness
your best revenge is to live your life *well-lived*

Questions of Soul Surfing
Outer Banks, North Carolina

Can one wave sincerely discern itself from another, distinct from rhythmic symphony heaving in from all corners of the world? can bony ankles and knees dissolve into sand and sky? do spirits ascend, whole, *atman,* when bodies die, as Hindus believe? once we realize "I" eternal, our fear of death fades away? or/and when the time comes for our bodies to die, is there is no "I" to transcend, no-thing to mourn or lose, as Buddhists say? once we realize eternal *no self,* our fear of death disappears? Can Great Mystery have one ethereal eye in water and one on dry land? is there only *One True Surf?* or are all maritime mysteries, above and below, folded into an eclectic playlist to tap dance to at sea's biggest jamboree? is what matters that you rsvp? do all swells, no matter where they roll from, eventually make their way home? Does God shake Her head at our stubborn contention over which is the *right* curl as we stand over shiny waxed boards lifeless on hot shore while we shout at the sun and each other, missing the sea for the waves?

Rachel Carson Wildlife Refuge, Maine

We saunter along her sea breath nests
her refuge of migratory waterfowl
her treasure of a place, warm inhale of
pine needles, salt marsh, kestrel hawks
cool exhale of seaweed, tidepools, rock
jagged edges along rugged shores
surge break, listen to pocketknife
whistles of gulls at low tide
imagine this scientist looking,
leaning, observing with sandpaper palms
as the sea hums secrets
as songbirds warble
witchery, witchery

she wrote *there may be consequences*
when we interfere with nature

toxic masculine atom split
nuclear fallout of chemical industry cries:
What unmarried childless female cares about the
future? (she raised three children, ~~does it matter~~)
too emotional too hysterical!
to notice fog trucks and dust squads
spraying insecticide confetti with singsong cheer
in parks, on beaches, schools, and streets
"Good for meeeeeee" but not for the
songbirds or salmon

maybe not for you or me either
she wrote *because we just do not know*

what affect they may have
Ms. Carson suggested,
years from now in mothers' milk
in babies' teeth
the world could not ignore the
open wounds left by low tides
infants born with hands on top of their
shoulders, trunks sprouted with little
feet, how much longer can we conceal
what we do to the air, water, and trees
we do to us, how much longer of
profits over people

How long does it take to break down?
Ms. Carson persisted
for this pitch forks
raised to break her
like the eagles' thin
chemical cracked eggshells

if she could take a big yellow taxi
here, she could see
not much has changed
not much has changed
still foolish manufactured boundaries
politics, poison sprays

what can we do? we would ask her
other than help our children wonder
show them how
to pay attention
to leaves who curl
up their edges
like teacups before it rains

Would she say, *yes, this exactly*
show them why it is *the most*
important thing
when the hummingbird, oriole, bobwhite
sing *witchery, witchery* each
symphonic spring

Red Nashville

their hand curves quietly
        around arc of your waist
                pulls you away from the drunks
                    closer to them

eases you behind the round table
        whiskey sticky, settle in
                awareness of heat where they hesitate
                    then relax against black smooth

drape of your worn jeans
        ardent surge flushes
                of what you could be together
                    without arguments or fights

without insecurity or invented infidelity
        understood flawless moment of suggested potential
                under red twinkle lights
                    while hopefuls in cowboy boots

and skeletal singers in 10-gallon hats scream
        for their break over the silver
                industrial bar blocking the
                    tiny half-moon stage

but neither of you notice any of this
        exchange no words, afraid to disturb
                the fluttered decision you both made
                    to leave their hand cupped over your hip, still aflame

Redwoods, California

have you inhaled heated earth spoors
exhaled by ancient forests? have your
eyes trailed thick bark rivers, higher
and higher, to beckon branches who
ebb through canopy of sun-filtered
leaves? you, a defenseless, green
baby, crawl in our sacred room of
your elders, only crests of massive,
shined shoes under swaying shins
visible. have you measured *3,000*
years of history, other than our
rings heaved to a slumped side? have
you calculated one of us alone uses
our toe's roots to pull *300* gallons
of soil's nutrients up to our most
revered leaves to alchemize into *400*
cubic feet of oxygen? child, we are
a grove of sentient wizards. have
you heard of the girl, yes girl, who
climbed into sister Luna, one of the
largest in our family, marked with
blue X of imminent destruction?
she sat for a day, stayed for *738*,
as Luna gave consent as her sticky
monkey feet gripped her syrupy
limbs, to peer at forests within
forests. moss, ferns, foxes, squirrels,
banana slugs, spotted owls, mothers
within Mother, as storms howled,
as she sprouted a silver streak in
23-year-old hair, as men sent riotous
helicopter blades to *knock her out,*

megaphones to *shout what they would do to her.* the same they had done, the same they *still do* to us: assault, pillage, dominate, break. a lucidity is birthed in conditions as these, a clear mission, not of superheroes, but of those courageous enough to care, respect their elders, share the stories that will save our lives, know when to climb to the top, when to grip tightly, when to sit in stillness to tap into deep reserves of patience, to grow strong roots like us.

so, yes, superheroes.

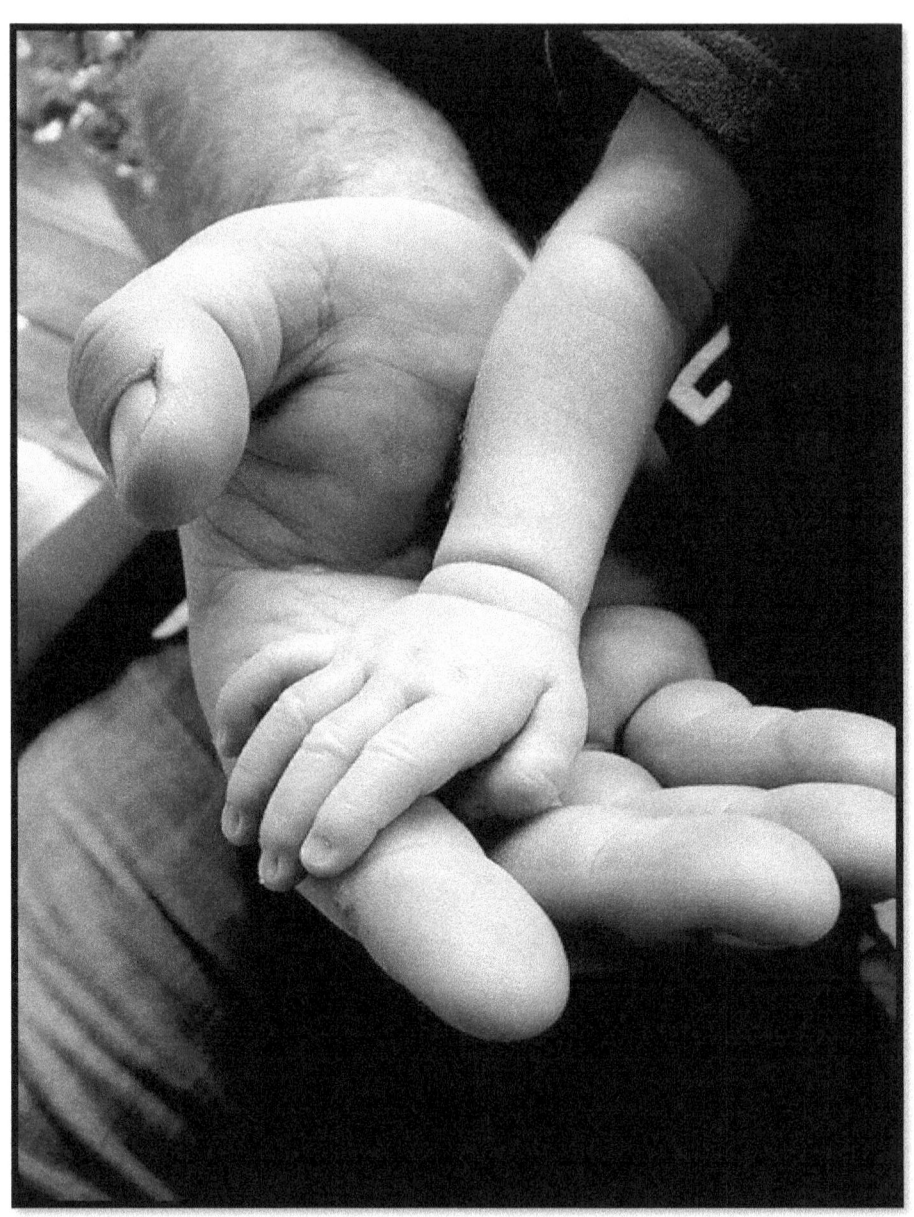

Rinse Repeat Chalkboard

After Mrs. Mann's whiteboard list of schools, Haslett High

kids shot at school thoughts and prayers sad face emojis online debates not the guns it is the guns
shake our heads go back to work back to school crickets chirp congress does nothing live in fear
kids shot at school thoughts and prayers sad face emojis online debates not the guns it is the guns
shake our heads go back to work back to school crickets chirp congress does nothing live in fear
kids shot at school thoughts and prayers sad face emojis online debates not the guns it is the guns
shake our heads go back to work back to school crickets chirp congress does nothing live in fear
kids shot at school thoughts and prayers sad face emojis online debates not the guns it is the guns
shake our heads go back to work back to school crickets chirp congress does nothing live in fear
kids shot at school thoughts and prayers sad face emojis online debates not the guns it is the guns
shake our heads go back to work back to school crickets chirp congress does nothing live in fear
kids shot at school thoughts and prayers sad face emojis online debates not the guns it is the guns
shake our heads go back to work back to school crickets chirp congress does nothing live in fear
kids shot at school thoughts and prayers sad face emojis online debates not the guns it is the guns
shake our heads go back to work back to school crickets chirp congress does nothing live in fear
kids shot at school thoughts and prayers sad face emojis online debates not the guns it is the guns
shake our heads go back to work back to school crickets chirp congress does nothing live in fear
kids shot at school thoughts and prayers sad face emojis online debates not the guns it is the guns
shake our heads go back to work back to school crickets chirp congress does nothing live in fear
kids shot at school thoughts and prayers sad face emojis online debates not the guns it is the guns
shake our heads go back to work back to school crickets chirp congress does nothing live in fear
kids shot at school thoughts and prayers sad face emojis online debates not the guns it is the guns
shake our heads go back to work back to school crickets chirp congress does nothing live in fear
kids shot at school thoughts and prayers sad face emojis online debates not the guns it is the guns
shake our heads go back to work back to school crickets chirp congress does nothing live in fear
kids shot at school thoughts and prayers sad face emojis online debates not the guns it is the guns
shake our heads go back to work back to school crickets chirp congress does nothing live in fear
kids shot at school thoughts and prayers sad face emojis online debates not the guns it is the guns
shake our heads go back to work back to school crickets chirp congress does nothing live in fear
kids shot at school thoughts and prayers sad face emojis online debates not the guns it is the guns
shake our heads go back to work back to school crickets chirp congress does nothing live in fear
kids shot at school thoughts and prayers sad face emojis online debates not the guns it is the guns
shake our heads go back to work back to school crickets chirp congress does nothing live in fear
kids shot at school thoughts and prayers sad face emojis online debates not the guns it is the guns
shake our heads go back to work back to school crickets chirp congress does nothing live in fear

Salem, Massachusetts

Crooked, bony digits tightly convinced
certainly, pointedly, decidedly
graha, graha

tangible terror in stony panted breath
summoned from accusations of conjured
confessions to avoid death

lit fires of reprimand, but it was ropes that consumed
Nineteen of them, twisted, and rocks, how many? enough to press
a full-grown man into stillness

Hung and pressed, Hung and pressed
Hung and pressed into
Lucifer's laundry line

fastened macabre clothespins with bitter
frostbit fingers from their coldest winter
licked their festered wounds

the faithful, the outsiders, all it took
a birthmark, dream, rumor, prickly sensation,
dead cattle, missed sermon, odor, inclination

to stack spectral evidence like pressed rocks
to put a four-year-old girl in goal, no chains small enough
to clasp around her baby bird wrists

her jailed mother lost her own belly's swell
Hysteria, planted with poisoned seeds,
a wicked crop to harvest

what begets an entire village
to fall to their calloused knees
to fulfill their own superstitions of evil deeds?

mold in the grain? suffocated existence?
cold, starvation?
isolation, homesickness?

long under gravestones split by massive elms
blame the victim charges past the village, across the land
societal incantations, ropes still on hand

San Andres Mountains

face presses cold

        cheek to rumbling van

                window, a.m. cerulean hour

opaque fog lifts

        first strands of sunrise's colors

                revealing luminous ancient

silent silhouettes

        mountain matriarchs

                rising for morning vespers

Seattle

Puget Sound
draw bridge
horn blows
space needle

hipster in green t-shirt:
"pickles are cucumbers soaked in evil"

public square
fresh tulips
raw salmon
tied and thrown

find bridge to jig dance under
troll's bulbous nose

Jinkx Monsoon
BenDeLaCreme
Pearl Jam, Nirvana
Soundgarden

flannel notes breastfed on
milky mists of sodden wind

Sex Appeal of an El Camino

An El Camino is what happens
when a truck makes sweet,
dirty love to a station wagon
while Lynyrd Skynyrd plays on the 8track
or Led Zeppelin's *Kashmir*

An El Camino is a coupe, a muscle car
a Chevrolet with rear wheel drive, pick up classified
swivel bucket or notchback bench seats
vinyl striped patterns, you can pick up just about anyone
if you have an El Camino

An El Camino is V-shaped
like the smooth geese heading to Mexico
like its revved big block engine
like the space between my legs
capital "V" capital "EL"

An El Camino is Prince if he were a seductive utility
steel bed, smooth grille, side skirts
carpeted door panels, stylized suspension upgrade
woodgrain panel trim, plush upholstery, Cam shaft
hydraulic front bumper, copious V6 or V8

An El Camino is four generations
of trial and error, invention and reinvention
utility and impracticality, of ironic self-awareness legacy
a vehicle, when someone demands, *are you a car or are you a truck?*
takes a drag of its cigarette, eyebrows raised, and exhales, *both.*

Sleepy Hollow

I just want my head back, nocturnally maddened in moonlight, he blazes past splintered schoolhouse windows welded with arithmetic pages and history books

Hugged into inland sea's cackling brook winds whisper strange spells under stone bridge, in eaves of old Dutch church, Autumn evenings' undressed limbs

Inelegant Ichabod, schoolmaster of superstition, somewhat selfish scarecrow coveting any pretty peach, particularly Katrina's estate, little ankles, and dainty feet

Whistling past pumpkin bellies rounding   winding path, horse hooves crunching hollow's withered leaves, every swallow, whippoorwill, and rustle a haunted bellow

Ominous omens, bizarre tales, trees of captivity spin and settle in Crane's weedy mind, mooring specter of Revolutionary War soldier, cloaked horseman riding

Rumors of musket or cannonball clipped in gruesome battle, each night, he and his shadowed stallion gallop, grasping severed fireball head aside the smoky saddle

Vanished, Ichabod disappeared like mist, his unsaddled horse at ease munching grass, nothing left behind save a broken pitch pipe and Cotton Mather's *History of Witchcraft*

Without a beat, Katrina's pretty feet dance under her wedding gown, cheers to Brom Bones, in his dashing fox tail hat, slinging mischief and merriment all over Tarrytown

Snuff Clouds in South Carolina

Southern Baptist Jesus hung in the hallway
Me-ma smelled of Irish spring and fresh powder
fleshy arms, clean and soft as baby legs, hands that rolled
biscuits in the army bowl, hands that cooked collard
greens and boiled peanuts from the Piggly Wiggly, "the Pig"
she called it, hands that dried and tied tobacco from the fields
snapped string beans under pine trees, hands that dipped peach
snuff, powdery brown clouds lingered from each laugh as she
passed gas in morse code across her chicken fried kitchen
hands that stirred aprons and stiff shirts in lye with a long
wooden stick in the cast iron black cauldron
her granddaughter's hands now fill every May
with purple petunias and yellow marigolds
Lord have mercy

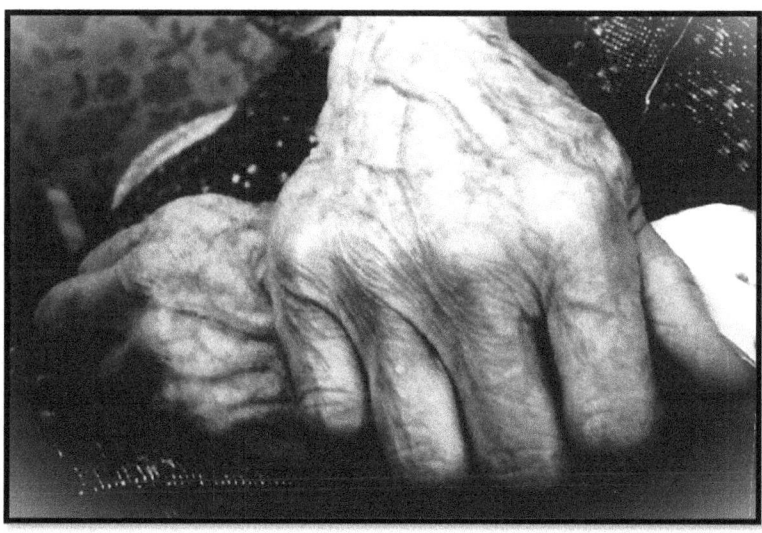

South Dakota (Rapid City)

This is how you became the father he would never be
    you built your ramshackle raft and rolled right over his turbulent
murky water leached from his acid anger-ravaged leaves

You, spotted fawn of frigid drenched winters, fiery parched summers
    little boy of *Paha Sapa*, sworn safeguarding, promised protection, cataclysmal
rampage surged in veins of snakes disguised as giants, land and childhood swallowed whole

You, monolith who pulled chocks, sailed your Appalachian cornbread heart
    through Arabian Sea to Suez, far away from his vicious Rushmore, his broken treaties
decades of black water battle memories, yet three times over, you emerged free

You, Orion who helps locate other stars, true luminous blue supergiant
    suctioned out the venom of locked darkness, forged your shoulders of swords
stitched your heart and hands into years of packed lunches, school projects, sewed

costumes, voice characters, built bunkbeds, scattered scavenger hunts, fixed stuffies,
    lego builds, library trips, and every single morning you've waved to them
as they climbed the yellow bus stairs, you became the father he could never be

*Paha Sapa *are the sacred Black Hills, land illegally taken through the broken Ft.
Laramie Treaty.*

Ultralight over the Mississippi River

It is time
to make our way down the cliff
of the mudslide
we call his last year

Past the broken limbs and
lost debris of each
agonized stage
of his drift further out to slush sea

It is time
to find the unsullied layers
to rest my feet
my chest, my face

To remember strata of
Chocolate malts (not shakes)
Chevys (never Fords)
Coca-Cola and a cigarette in the mornings (no Pepsi)

How it felt to soar with wings at dusk
weave over the meandering Mississippi
cornfields whistling
Tom Petty tunes

The post-it-note from my
'92 Toyota Corolla wagon
when I crossed Ohio's border
for good:

"Please remember
To change my oil, Love Toyota" in his
mechanic's careful, small letters

The familiar car grease scent
passed through his Carhartt jacket
when he hugged you

His timbred voice
when he said "sweetheart"
so tenderly, like the low
crackle of a long-tended fire

(The) United States of this Body
(An American Psalm)

This body is rattle, snakeskin shed to earth.
This body is underground bunker, tent, and yurt.

This body is tree trunk, roots, thick branches stretched,
imperfectly filled with perfectly twined nests.

This body is sparrow and sinew, spleen, and sanctuary.
This body is *Gemara* and gospel, epistle, and elegy.

This body is tongue coated red, white, and blue, untied shoes.
This body just wants to age with grace, becoming its own muse.
This body is milk…letdown cream, catfish mouth and baby breath,
      Proverb, Psalm, love letter, and lament.

This body is overpass, bridge, and tunnel
      sunken ship, and highway vixen vessel,
      billboards that warn, "Hell is Real."

This body is pox, virus, and compost covering.
This body is regenerating as it is hibernating.
This body is detour ahead, under construction,
      covenant, sworn oath, independence declaration

This body is Land of Enchantment, Prairie, and Garden State,
      wheat, soybean, corn, and fingers tobacco stained.
This body is daffodil and daisy, sunflower and magnolia.
      Sequoia and sycamore, sweet gum, and catalpa.

This body is red-winged blackbird and cardinal,
        cactus blossom and waterfall.
This body *flies with her own wings*, heart of it all.

This body is Red River, Rio Grande, and Shenandoah,
    cracked pavement, dusty miles, and dirt roads.
This body is maple syrup on tap, sugarshack.
This body is coal dusted canary of this country's mineshaft.

This body is broken treaties, broken vows, and broken teeth.
This body is rushing waters, maps of tributaries.
This body is shushed mouths, erased herstories.
This body is trauma on trauma on trauma on repeat.
This body is love my country, not my government.

This body is on its knees, not for some man, but rising a mother's pleas
for her children to go to school each morning and come back alive.

This body is sick of being mansplained, man-lawed, and colonized.
This body writhed and cried, scrapped, and survived.

This body is tired of being told to smile when she don't *feel* like it,
    days when it takes volcano strength to hide it.

This body is folklore, fairytale, urban legend, and fan fiction.
    liberation, emancipation, *natural* rights, not just given.
This body is broken systems.
        Coins flipped into fountains.
        More valleys than mountains.
        More turquoise than gold.
        More shadow than smoke.
        More clay than sky.
        More funnel cake than apple pie.

This body is po' boys and grits, cobb salad and deep dish.

This body is pueblo, holler, and hill, bison, bear, elk and eagle.
This body is *we the people*.
This body is Hindu, Muslim, Buddhist, Christian,
    Sikh, Jewish, Baha'i and Pagan,
        believer, sinner, seeker washed clean, bhakti, devotee, image of Divinity.

This body is your body This body is my body
This body is poetry   slingshot into the void.

This body is imbalanced scales, cradled in a Borderless Palm,
whistling her wild and weary,
                              centuries old American Psalm.

U.P. Gold, Michigan

Up in the Upper Peninsula
rivers run like honey
golden as the sun's belly

Glacial, amber torrents
pour over bold rocks
heavy as Yooper accents

She squats in the dewy morning
peers under a navy baseball hat
bulge of belly hammock

She parts the bramble plants
with hummingbird speed
swiftly plucks delicate plum spheres

Forest shades of emerald, juniper, moss, pine
glide into shock of cold, rust colored
liquid slides over sticky summer skin

earth mound, her Venus form
surfaces, floats as if untethered
in a water lullaby

Vietnam Memorial, Washington, D.C.

The Wall . is much smaller . than in pictures . like seeing the Mona Lisa . in front of your . nose . not as grandiose . as painted in the mind . not stretching up like the shiny . WW II . monument . reaching with its muscular fountains . and erect statues . No . this wall . hunkers down . on its haunches . in the dirt . smoking a pall mall . bushy yellowed . moustache . remembering . wet highlands of Pleiku . rockets . like can openers . peeling . roofs . off barracks . craters . the size of houses . overturned giants . in the wet mud of . strange earth . if you could hear the whistle . you still had a few moments . to get to the . bunkers . silence meant it was on top of you . too close . remembering . your throbbing . heel at sunrise . looking down . hunks of skin shrapnel sliced away . you can lose a lot of . blood . before the medics . start to panic . unbearable humidity closing in on young lung . branches . mud climbing up platoon shins . rain, always, rain every day . full moon pregnant . washee girl who squatted down . knees high . rinsing soldiers clothes each day . one . afternoon she left . gave birth . returned the next morning . squatting . washing . remembering . villagers in conical hats . formed by dried leaves and bamboo sticks . silk wrap dresses . VC ground attack . carrying rockets . on their backs . no uniforms . Barber Charlie down . WW II "spookies" . hosed the night sky . with bright red traces . like squirting blood . half dome devastation . in the daylight . through the filmy windows . soldiers played kid . pirated reel to reel . Beach Boys . Bread . Beatles . Rare Earth . original mixtapes . pretending to be home .

Waffle House
Paducah, Kentucky

orange earrings dangle
shaped like pears
approach the wiped
table, egg yolk
Pollock splashed across
greasy nametag, *Peach*
 "How do you
want your omelet,
sweetheart?" *cheese…please*
Peach nods, earrings
swinging *…little dash*
of love, weary
endless road miles
Peach's mauve lipstick
corners rise, "Honey,
I'm the momma
to seven kiddos,
not a problem."
on the way
from, this way
to any destination
story, location, black
coffee this Thursday
night, steaming sturdy
Mother of seven
port in storm

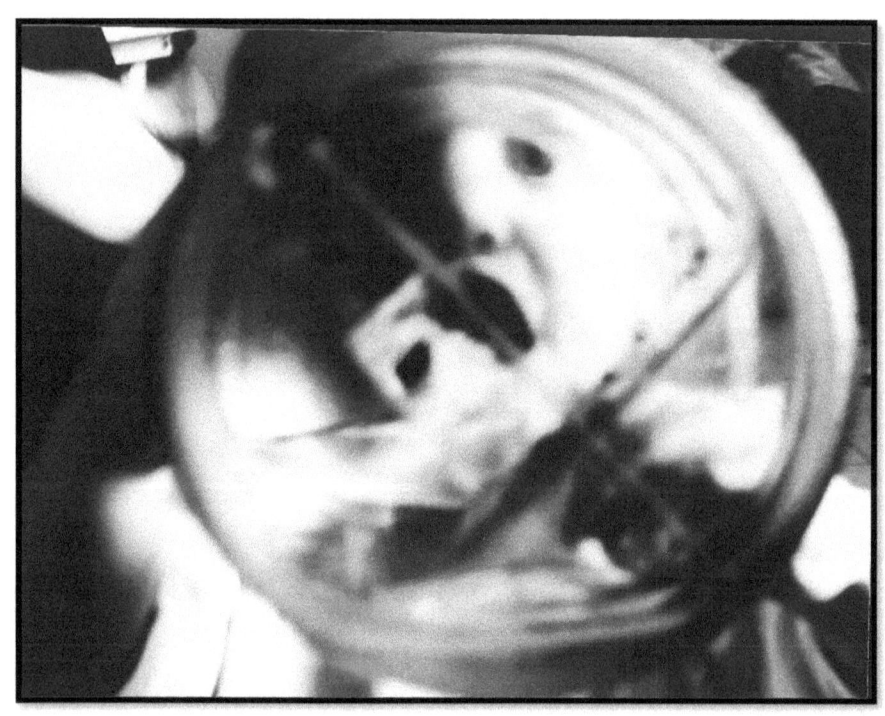

Watching Ukraine

this world is loud
a percussion of restless tongues
our thoughts are loud
      rowdy, flawed, and exhausting

here is an invitation
to remember we are more
than this unfiltered chaos
      than our compulsive inner spiraling

collectively, we watch, and we wait
a stunning David push back a relentless Goliath
watch compulsively, intensively, helplessly
      as insulated voyeurs

because we know
this could be us; *this could be us*
and we have to ask, would we have this grit
      this unwavering resistance

against such terror
and insatiable snuffing of life
against such desensitized destruction
      and cloaked fury

what is there to do
but sing our mourning songs
and estranged praises
      with our clumsy protests and cracked wings

what is there to do
but refuse to ever ignore
Hey, what's that sound
       and hold vigil for what is in shreds

what is there to do
except to look at each other wholly
and utter *my God, my God*
       as the psalmists did

to whisper *my humanity, my humanity*
if we just had today
what would you be anchored by
       what sun would turn your face toward

what would you give away without hesitation
what precious words would you choose
and who would you give them to
       if we just had today

would you be a mirror
or a catalyst
in stillness, in focus
       on your heart, *your heart*

when the rock and rubble slide and break
you dig into your edged truth
stretch and reach down into
       your exposed gnarled roots

dive low into your deep pockets
of hope folded and unfolded
because this damaged world is loud
       but our bruised, tender hearts can be

                         louder

West Virginia Train Tracks

we dance by the horizontal ladder
moon full, high above us, luminous
near the hill obscured gorge

you sing *loud*
until the horn blows louder
gritty rumble of

ta ta ta ta ta ta ta
drowns out your words
as you invite me into

blushed midnight
your mountain lip liner notes
soundlessly serenade into mine

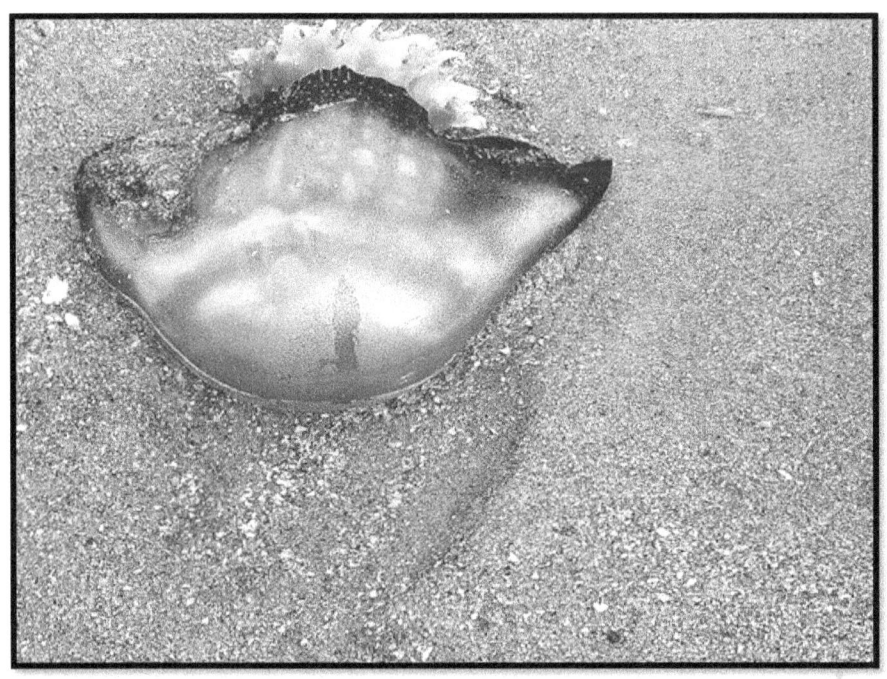

Whale Watching off the Coast of Maine

Earthworms thud faint staccato sounds
Whale songs travel thousands of miles
Through underwater infinity
Impersonal, indifferent
Massive, not malevolent
Coiled power of unleashed havoc
Under glassy halcyon surface
Pffffft alerts to long anticipated
Somehow still sudden
Emergence
Gray alien ship form
Sea unicorn of mysteries
Rises like Haystack Rock
Do not blink,
Slaps back through the waters
Submerges into oblivion once again
Even their massive shapes seem
Pocket-sized pebbles against an infinite
Water world, empty of horizons
Fins flip, initiate waves for long
journey to unrevealed hushed shoreline
Where someone digs their toes in the sand
Red sandals dangle off their right index finger
Above elastic mouths of writhing earthworms

Who Dat

a *Who Dat*
is a plywood flat
splintering 8track
four static speakers
bungee tied
one on each side
flowing downriver
PBRs and Coors
sweating spires
of a lil' blue cooler
audio kingdom
tethered to sweltering
inner tube
gummed underneath
sunburnt knees
feet dangling
over jumping catfish
current of lazy eddies
dodging fishing line
in snapped tangles
cast off, still
bobbing in this muddy water
made of moonshine

Woods of Wisconsin

shedding soft skins each conversation
      hours of exchange into shooting stars
vaporing into ethereal constellations

chilled walks, night's breeze blowing
      static through the receiver, relishing
what's good for immortal and stellar souls

volleys of Augustine, Aquinas, Bible
      and Bowie, papers of politics and religion
all that is forbidden to deliberate, at the table

no agenda, true colors fleshed out in unguarded space
      no bitter entanglements, geography a helper
against us, leaving only our celestial bodies, astral debates

breathing life back where numbness had gripped
      clutched heavy talons gently began to release
to *remember* how it feels to drink deeply, to live

God as protector, we shared polydreams
      rigid shards, witness of stars, night sky
luminous, still held in holy orbs of your rosary

World's Largest Roadside Attraction

massive mailbox, hammer, and whistle
thirty-foot pistachio, peanut, and pencil

colossal cuckoo clock, birdcage, immense windchimes
towering thermometer, teapot, behemoth ball of twine

considerable cheese wheel, wooden whopper of a rocking chair
one red and white striped "Catsup" bottle, 170 feet in the air

what is better than bigger? a biggest that *works*
a two-ton frying pan that can fry chicken is a surprising perk

while the tiny town of Ishpeming boasts two performing goliaths
a firing 400-pound rifle known as *Big Ernie*, a 23-foot running chainsaw named *Big Gus*
                              nothing to worry about, not at all dangerous

hefty erected epic exaggerations give amusement galore and make tourists swoon
our own illusions as giants exposed in the quiet yearning to be the little spoon

Yosemite 1

Half dome unmoving
climber a scatter of dust
Who are they kidding?

Yosemite 2

We slept under stars
pulled possibilities of
crystal clear vast stretch
fingertips still out of reach
of God, of infinity

Zora Neale Hurston! Eatonville, Florida

1.

I wish I could have known Zora Neale Hurston!
raised on guava, grapefruit, and boiled eggs
rattlesnakes, alligators, and Florida wildness
lurking in shadows of sharp edges as she
perched on the gatepost, neck elongated
to hop along with a traveler to Orlando
enough to gather a story, a spell down the road
lingering at Joe Clarke's general store
catching all the pieces of happenings
swapping and spitting
Iron teakettles whistling

2.

I wish I could have known Zora Neale Hurston!
she spoke with the trees
ran with the moon
jumped at the sun
all present solely for delight of her company
she dreamed of the world from her chinaberry tree
letters and words winged ribbons
her expansive mind gave her climb onto
long, lifted tails of mockingbirds
shocking visions coming to fruition
feet tingled with wandering dust
always felt like a "crow" in pigeons' nest
circled the south with camera,
pen and pearl-handled revolver tucked under
collecting stories of folks steeped
in the tannin of being human
songs, games, gossip, courtships
rituals, rhymes, recipes, myths

as she knew cosmic secrets hid
in mule bones masked as mundane

3.
I wish I could have known Zora Neale Hurston!
she became blood tied
in sympathetic magic - hoodoo
she lay, supple navel against roughness of rattlesnake skin
for 3 days and 3 nights, the *nzazi* line
Congo lightning bolt on curved flesh of her back
mark of power, symbol of light
and because she saw Divine Love's many forms
belted out Baptist hymns with her roadside African Church of God
Spirit appearing in the rhythm She pleases
Uncontained, like…

4.
Zora Neale Hurston!
(those who knew her, did they realize?)
rooted down in the hills of Haiti like a Catalpa tree
when a crashing, inside out love exchange
poured through her heart's branches
into Tea Cake, into Janie Mae
and in the autumn of her life
this award winning, passport filled
dynamite Guggenheim recipient's
novels were out of print
when she peeled off this world's body
scars, marks, hung them up like a robe
spirit ascending, body laid in an unmarked grave
until Alice Walker, *as long as we're wishing,*
wish I could know her too,
laced up her traveling shoes collecting clues
as Spirit led her to wade
through waist-high thistle, knotweed, plantain
stepped over snakes in an unmarked search
until her foot found forgiving earth

planted a new mark of power: *"Genius - of - the - South"*
and Zora's books came back to life
back into laps belonging to minds
transformed by a woman ascribed
to the anguish of *"bearing an untold story inside."*

5.
I wish I could have known Zora Neale Hurston!
she had a dog named Prince
offered to send her toenails to debate her critics
wore hats, slacks, and ties
often entered a room to announce:
"Queen Zora has arrived."

I wish I could have known Zora Neale Hurston
well enough to ask her how she heaved the horizon
over her cleaved shoulder, and how she leaned into a
life that calls us, and still, right now…
calls us
to come see

About the Author

Hayden is the current Poet Laureate for Sinclair College and an award-winning Professor of Humanities, Philosophy, and World Religions. A *River Heron Review* Editors' Prize Winner and *Pushcart Prize* Nominee, Hayden is a Mama and animal rescuer who lives on a windy little farm with her family and many furry rescue babies, including a blind, three-legged "angel in a dog suit" named Vinny Valentine. She loves words, nature, and El Caminoes.

American Saunter is her debut collection.

Follow the Author:

Website: https://windychickenpoet.com/
Facebook: https://www.facebook.com/WindyChickenPoet/
Instagram: https://www.instagram.com/windychickenpoet/

References

"To Saunter" John Muir Quote
> Palmer, Albert W., *The Mountain Trail and Its Message*, The Pilgrim Press, *1911.*

City Lights, San Francisco
> *"…those who explode like Roman candles"* inspired by Kerouac, Jack, *On the Road,* Penguin Classics, 1999.

Grand Canyon
> *"sound your barbaric yawp"* from Whitman, Walt, *Song of Myself, 52, Leaves of Grass,* Norton, 1973; *Beauty Before Me…*(Beauty Prayer) *Walk in Beauty* Prayer, Navajo/Dine

Mansfield, Missouri (Home of Laura Ingalls Wilder)
> *"This could not be forgotten because now is now…it can never be a long time ago."* Little House in the Big Woods, Harper and Brothers, 1932

No Volvere Amor Mio (Tri-State Tea Readings)
> *"No Volvere Amor Mio"* Gipsy Kings, *Este Mundo*, Elektra Records, 1991
>
> *"Open sky of crystal silence…"* by Foss, Sam Walter, *Songs of the Average Man,* Lothrop, Lee & Shepard Co, Boston, 1907

Rachel Carson Wildlife Refuge, Maine
> *"witchery witchery"* from *"witchity, witchity,"* Lawlor, Laurie, and Laura Beingessner, *Rachel Carson and Her Book that Changed the World,* Holiday House, 2012.

Rinse Repeat Chalkboard
> inspired by Mrs. Mann's whiteboard school list, Haslett High, Social Media; permission given by Mrs. Mann to author directly to rework as found poetry

This World is Loud (Watching Ukraine)
"*hey, what's that sound*" from *For What It's Worth (Stop, Hey What's That Sound)*, Stephen Sills, Buffalo Springfield, Dec 5, 1966, Atco Records.

(The) United States of this Body (An American Psalm)
"*flies with her own wings*" (Oregon state motto); "*heart of it all*" (Ohio state slogan).

Zora Neale Hurston! Eatonville, Florida
"*There is no agony like bearing...; Queen Zora has arrived...calls us to come see*" from Hurston, *Zora Neale, Dust Tracks on a Road*, HarperCollins Publishers, 2006 and *Zora Neale Hurston: Jump at the Sun*, S22, EP 2: American Masters, 2008

Acknowledgments

First and always to God/Great Mystery, *thank you* is my prayer every single day.

Heidi Arnold, Nadine Cichy, Heather Johnson-Taylor, Sally Lahmon, Kimberly Rickard, Lindsey Slanker, Derek Petrey, and Nora Stanger for invaluable initial input in the first draft. Jason Blakely at *Poetry is Life* for publishing my first poem, your kindness, and authenticity. Douglas Sovonick for your generosity of time and immense talent in creating the perfect cover. Robyn (Dumpster B), Emily, C, Beth, Lauren, Deb, Kathleen, Judy - my joyful lady cheer team. John Dorsey, Aimee Noel, Cathryn Essinger, and Teresa Berkowitz for your beautiful blurbs. Angela Yuriko Smith for being such an enthusiastic cheer section through this whole journey. Furaha Henry-Jones - Queen! Mother! Alchemist! Can you ever know what you mean to me? Jamey Coyote Dunham whose wisdom made this stronger; your support keeps me swimming. Amber Tamblyn, for writing about why women should trust their intuition...always.

Sweetheart Sikh *Days Inn* clerk, wherever you are, thank you for your compassion and burrito. Kris Coffey, Marcy Vonderwell, and J.R. Jamison for your time, talent, and great advice. Melissa and Ed Burkley, thirty years of friendship still going strong, I love you both. John Muir, for teaching me how to saunter and Rev. Dr. Barbara Battin, for teaching me peace. *Meadowlark Press* for choosing *American Saunter* as a semi-finalist for the *Birdy Poetry Prize*.

Thank you Lindsay and Jonas from https://itsacharminglife.com/ for taking time to read and give such charming feedback on *Sleepy Hollow*. Eric Paul Shaffer, whose *RattleSnake Rider* opened my little writer's heart when I was 14, and whose support 30+ years later is proof magic exists. Edward Vidaurre, Avery Castillo, Priscilla Celina Suarez, and *FlowerSong Press* FOREVER for having faith in me and my first book. Jimmy, my favorite, for your unconditional love, father of the year (every year) mojo, and lifegiving humor. Our daughters, it is all for YOU, my big-time loves, to the moon and back, a bazillion times. Finally, *you,* readers of my first book, thank you for spending time with my heart.

The End

FLOWERSONG
PRESS

FlowerSong Press nurtures essential verse from, about, and throughout the borderlands. Literary. Lyrical. Boundless.

Sign up for announcements about
new and upcoming titles at:

www.flowersongpress.com

www.ingramcontent.com/pod-product-compliance
Lightning Source LLC
Chambersburg PA
CBHW050447150626
46551CB00029B/1980